Presented to ___Jack_____

by ___Mommy_____

on ___12/25/08_____

Text © 2004 The Livingstone Corporation. © 2004 Standard Publishing, Cincinnati, Ohio.
A division of Standex International Corporation. All rights reserved. Printed in China. Project
editor: Robin Stanley. Design: Robert Glover. Typesetting: Peggy Theile.

Produced with the assistance of The Livingstone Corporation (www.LivingstoneCorporation.com).
Project author: Jeanette Dall. Project consultant: Dr. Mary Manz Simon. Project staff: Betsy Todt
Schmitt, Dr. Bruce B. Barton, David R. Veerman, and Mary Horner Collins.

Scripture quotations taken from the Holy Bible, New Living Translation, copyright © 1996.
Used by permission of Tyndale House Publishers, Inc., Wheaton, Illinois 60189. All rights reserved.
New Living Translation and the New Living Translation logo are registered trademarks of Tyndale
House Publishers, Inc. NLT is a trademark of Tyndale House Publishers, Inc.

10 09 08 07 06 05   9 8 7 6 5 4 3 2

ISBN 0-7847-1597-1

Play-and-Learn
BIBLE

illustrated by Terry Julien

Standard
PUBLISHING
Bringing The Word to Life™

Cincinnati, Ohio

Table of Contents
Old Testament

New Testament

God Made Everything

Genesis 1:1–2:3

God made the and everything in it.

It was very dark. So God made light.

Then God made the on day 2.

On day 3 God made .

God also made lots and lots of plants.

world   sky   two   three   land

He made  and beautiful .

Then God made lights in the  .

The  to shine in the day.

The ☾ and ✦ to shine at night.

trees   flowers   sun   moon   stars

Next God made all kinds of

 and .

On day six God made animals.

Tall giraffes, slow  , and cuddly .

Then God made someone special.

birds   *fish*   *turtles*   *cats*

God made someone to him.

He made someone to take care of the  .

God made  .

God liked everything he made. Then he rested.

In the beginning God created the heavens and the earth.
Genesis 1:1, NLT

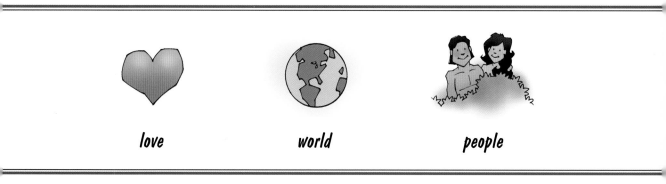

love   world   people

SAY: As I read the story, you do the motions.

The First People

Genesis 2:15-25; 3:20

God made a man from the dusty ground.

Pretend to make something with your hands.

Then God breathed into the man.

Take a deep breath and blow it out.

The man's name was Adam.

Say Adam's name three times.

God put Adam in a beautiful garden.

Move both arms in wide, sweeping motions.

God had the animals march past Adam.

Pretend to march in a parade.

Adam named each animal. What a lot of names!

Pretend to point to animals and name them.

But God saw that Adam still was lonely.

Shake your head and make a sad face.

11

So God made Adam go to sleep.

Pretend to sleep.

And he made a woman from one of Adam's ribs.

Point to your sides.

Adam was happy there was someone like him!

Clap your hands and make a happy face.

Adam called the woman Eve.

Say Eve's name three times.

He [God] made us, and we are his.

Psalm 100:3, NLT

13

SAY: As I read the story, you repeat the words in color and do the motions.

A Boat and a Rainbow

Genesis 6:14–8:19; 9:8-13

God told Noah to build a boat. A big, big boat.
Open arms wide.

Soon it will rain. Splish, splash! Splish, splash!
Wiggle your fingers and lower your hands to make rain.

Noah's family will be safe. Safe in the boat.
Hug yourself.

The animals came to the boat. Two by two.
Hold up two fingers.

God shut the boat's door. Bam! Bam!

Pretend to hammer.

It rained and rained. Forty days and nights.

Rapidly clap hands on legs.

Water covered everything. All the earth.

Spread hands wide.

But everyone on the boat was safe. Safe and dry.

Rub yourself dry.

15

The water stayed a long time.

A long, long time. *Nod your head.*

Soon God made the water go down.

Down, down. *Squat down.*

The boat landed on a mountain.

A tall, tall mountain. *Stand on tiptoes and stretch up.*

The animals came out.

Two by two. *Hold up two fingers.*

Noah's family came out. Hooray, hooray!
Jump up and down.

God protected them all. Thank you, God.
Pretend to pray.

God said, "No more big, big floods."
Shake head no.

God gave his promise. A rainbow for us!

You care for people and animals alike, O LORD.
Psalm 36:6, NLT

Joseph Forgives

Genesis 37:18-36; 41:37—45:15

Joseph's brothers were mean to him,
Mean to him, mean to him.
Joseph's brothers were mean to him;
They sold him as a slave.

One day the brothers went to Egypt,
Went to Egypt, went to Egypt.
One day the brothers went to Egypt,
Where Joseph lived and ruled.

They didn't know who Joseph was,
Joseph was, Joseph was.
They didn't know who Joseph was;
They came to buy some food.

When Joseph told them who he was,
Who he was, who he was.
When Joseph told them who he was,
They were really scared!

But Joseph said he loved them all,
Loved them all, loved them all.
But Joseph said he loved them all,
And forgave what they had done.

You must forgive others.
Colossians 3:13, NLT

Baby Moses

Exodus 1:22—2:10

There once was a bad king in Egypt.

He said, "Throw all the baby boys into the river."
  Put your hands to your face and shake your head no.

One mother hid her baby in the house.

But the baby grew too big to hide.
  Pretend to hide the baby.

The baby's mother made a basket boat.

She put the baby in the basket boat.
  Pretend to put the baby in a basket.

The mother put the basket in the river.

She hid it in the tall weeds along the shore.
  Pretend to carry the basket and put it down.

The baby's sister stayed and watched.

The king's daughter, a princess, came to the river.
  Pretend to hide and watch the princess.

The baby cried. The princess opened the basket and said, "This baby must be a Hebrew child."

Pretend to cry like a baby.

The sister went to the princess and said,

"Do you want someone to care for the baby?"

Pretend to hold and rock the baby.

The sister ran home and got the baby's mother.

The Hebrew mother took her baby home.

Pretend to carry the baby.

24

The baby grew older,
and the princess adopted him into her family.

Pretend to hug the baby.

The princess named the baby Moses.
God kept baby Moses safe.

He [God] cares about
what happens to you.
1 Peter 5:7, NLT

Moses and the Burning Bush

Exodus 3:1—4:31

Moses took care of  in the desert.

One day he saw a that was on .

But the did not burn up! "Amazing,"

said Moses. "Why isn't that burning

up? I must go over to see this." God's voice

sheep   *bush*   *fire*

called to Moses from the .

"Here I am," Moses answered. "Take off

your ," God said. This is special

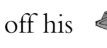 ." Moses was afraid so he took

off his and listened to God.

shoes   *ground*

God said, "Go and help my  escape

from Egypt." Moses asked, "Who, me? I can't

help your  ." Moses didn't think the

mean would listen to him. "Yes, you,"

God said. "Go, for I will be with you."

Moses asked, "What should I tell the ?"

people

God said, "Tell them that sent you.

Tell the I will lead them to a new

land. Then tell the that he must let my

go." So Moses went to Egypt and

God helped him.

God is my helper.
Psalm 54:4, NLT

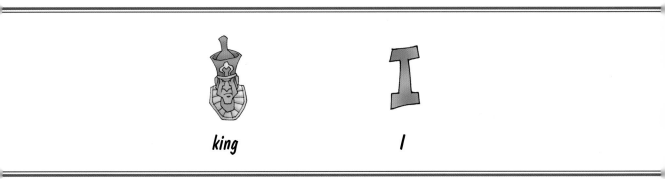

king   **I**

SAY: As I read the story, you do the motions.

Moses and the Red Sea

Exodus 13:17—15:21

Finally, the mean king in Egypt let the people go.

Pretend to be walking and walking.

God led them toward the new land.

Keep walking. Point straight ahead.

Soon the people came to the Red Sea.

Move hands to make wave motions.

But then the people heard loud sounds.

Put your hand behind your ear to listen.

The Egyptian army and chariots were coming.
Pretend to be driving a horse and chariot.

The people shivered with fear.
Pretend to be very scared.

They cried out to God, "Please help us!"
Pretend to be begging for help.

God told Moses, "Hold your staff over the water."
Pretend to hold a long stick out in front of you.

31

Then God made the wind blow.
Blow as hard as you can.

The wind moved the water of the Red Sea.
Put your hands together and then push them apart.

There was a dry path through the sea.
Pretend to look surprised and point.

The people walked through the sea.
Walk in place.

The Egyptian army followed.
Pretend to drive a horse and chariot.

God made the water come back together.

Spread your arms wide and bring them together.

The Egyptians drowned in the sea.

Stoop down and cover your head with your hands.

The people sang a song of thanks to God.

Clap your hands and pretend to be singing.

God will rescue his people.

Zechariah 9:16, NLT

God Gives the Ten Commandments

Exodus 19:1—20:17

Moses and the Israelites were camped by Mt. Sinai.
Put the tips of your fingers together to make a mountain.

Moses went up the mountain to talk to God.
Make your fingers walk.

There was lots of thunder and lightning.
Clap your hands; make zigzag lines with your fingers.

God gave Moses some rules for the people.
Hold hands together, palms up, like an open book.

The rules were called the Ten Commandments.
Hold up ten fingers.

Number 1 was "Worship only God."
Hold up one finger.

Number 2 was "Don't make any idols
to worship."
Hold up two fingers.

Number 3 was "God's name is special."
Hold up three fingers.

Number 4 was "Worship God and rest on
the Sabbath."
Hold up four fingers.

Number 5 was "Love and obey your parents."
Hold up five fingers.

Number 6 was "Do not hurt other people."
Hold up six fingers.

Number 7 was "Respect marriage."
Hold up seven fingers.

Number 8 was "Do not steal."
Hold up eight fingers.

Number 9 was "Tell the truth."
Hold up nine fingers.

Number 10 was "Be happy with what you have."
Hold up ten fingers.

Loving God means keeping his commandments.

1 John 5:3, NLT

The Battle of Jericho

Joshua 6:1-20

Jericho was a big city with high walls.
Reach as high as you can.

The big gates in the wall were locked.
Squeeze your hands tight together.

Joshua did not know how to get in.
Hold out your hands, palms up, and shake head no.

But God told Joshua what to do.
Point upward.

"March around the city for six days," God said.
March in place.

"And on the seventh day, the priests will blow horns." *March and pretend to blow a horn.*

So the people marched for six days.
March and hold up six fingers.

Each day they walked around Jericho one time.
March and hold up one finger.

Joshua said, "Don't say a word until I tell you to shout." *Hold a finger to your mouth and whisper, "Shhh."*

39

So the people did what Joshua said.
Pretend to march with finger to mouth.

On the seventh day, they got up very early.
Yawn and stretch.

This day they went around the city seven times.
March and hold up seven fingers.

On the seventh time around, the priests blew their horns. *Pretend to blow on a horn.*

Then Joshua said, "Shout! For the Lord has given you the city!" *Shout "Praise God!"*

The people shouted and the walls came falling down! *Raise your hands high and make them come down.*

Joshua's soldiers marched into Jericho.
Pretend to march over the fallen wall.

God helped them win the battle.
Raise both arms up as high as you can.

He [God] will give you victory!
Deuteronomy 20:4, NLT

God Helps Gideon

Judges 6:1–7:22

The farmers' wheat was stolen. Bad, bad enemies.

Wag finger back and forth.

The people of Israel prayed. "God please help us!"

Fold your hands in prayer.

An angel told Gideon, "Mighty hero,

God is with you."

Gideon blew a horn. Calling all soldiers!

Pretend to blow a horn.

Thousands of soldiers came. Too many men.

Hold hands out, palms up, and shake your head.

God said, "Send the men who are afraid home."

So Gideon said, "Go home."

Point with finger.

Many men stayed. Still too many men.

Hold hands out, palms up, and shake your head.

God said, "Bring them to the water.

Let them drink." *Kneel down.*

Some men drank from their hands.

Slurp, slurp. *Pretend to drink water from your hands.*

God said, "Take these 300 men.

I will give you victory." *Pump your fist into the air.*

43

Gideon gave each man a horn. Toot! Toot!

Pretend to blow a horn.

Gideon gave each man a torch inside a jar.

Hot! Hot! *Pretend to touch something hot.*

The enemies were sleeping. Snore, snore.

Pretend to sleep and snore.

Gideon's men blew their horns. Toot! Toot!

Pretend to blow a horn.

Gideon's men broke their jars.

Crack! Crack! *Pretend to break a jar on the ground.*

The men shouted,

"For the Lord and for Gideon!"

The enemies were scared and ran away.

Run, run! *Pretend to run in place.*

The LORD your God fights for you.
Joshua 23:10, NLT

Ruth Is Kind to Naomi

Ruth 1:1—2:23; 4:9-10

Naomi was  . Her husband and sons had

died. had been married to Naomi's son.

Naomi wanted to return . She told

to stay with her family. "I will stay with

you," said . Ruth Naomi.

sad   Ruth   home

Naomi and Ruth were too poor to buy food.

Ruth said, "Let me go out into the  .

I will gather  for you." Naomi said,

"All right, my daughter, go ahead."

Ruth  Naomi.

loved	field	grain

Ruth went to a  of .

She picked up leftover for food.

Boaz owned the . He was part of

Naomi's family. Boaz could see that

was kind to Naomi. Ruth Naomi.

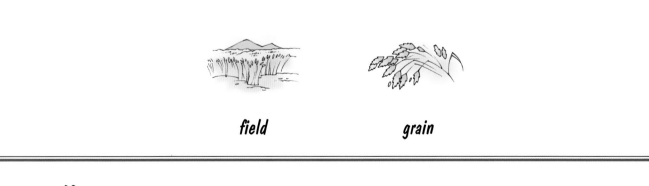

field   grain

He told Ruth, "Pick as much  as you want. Always stay in my _____." Boaz wanted to take care of and Naomi.

He married . Naomi lived in their with them. Ruth Naomi.

Be kind to each other.
Ephesians 4:32, NLT

Ruth   loved   home

SAY: Help me tell this story by pretending to be Samuel.

Samuel Listens to God

1 Samuel 3:1-19

Samuel was a young boy. He lived in the temple.

Samuel helped Eli, the priest.

One night, Samuel was sleeping.

Pretend to be sleeping.

Someone called, "Samuel!"

Samuel said, "Here I am."

Say, "Here I am."

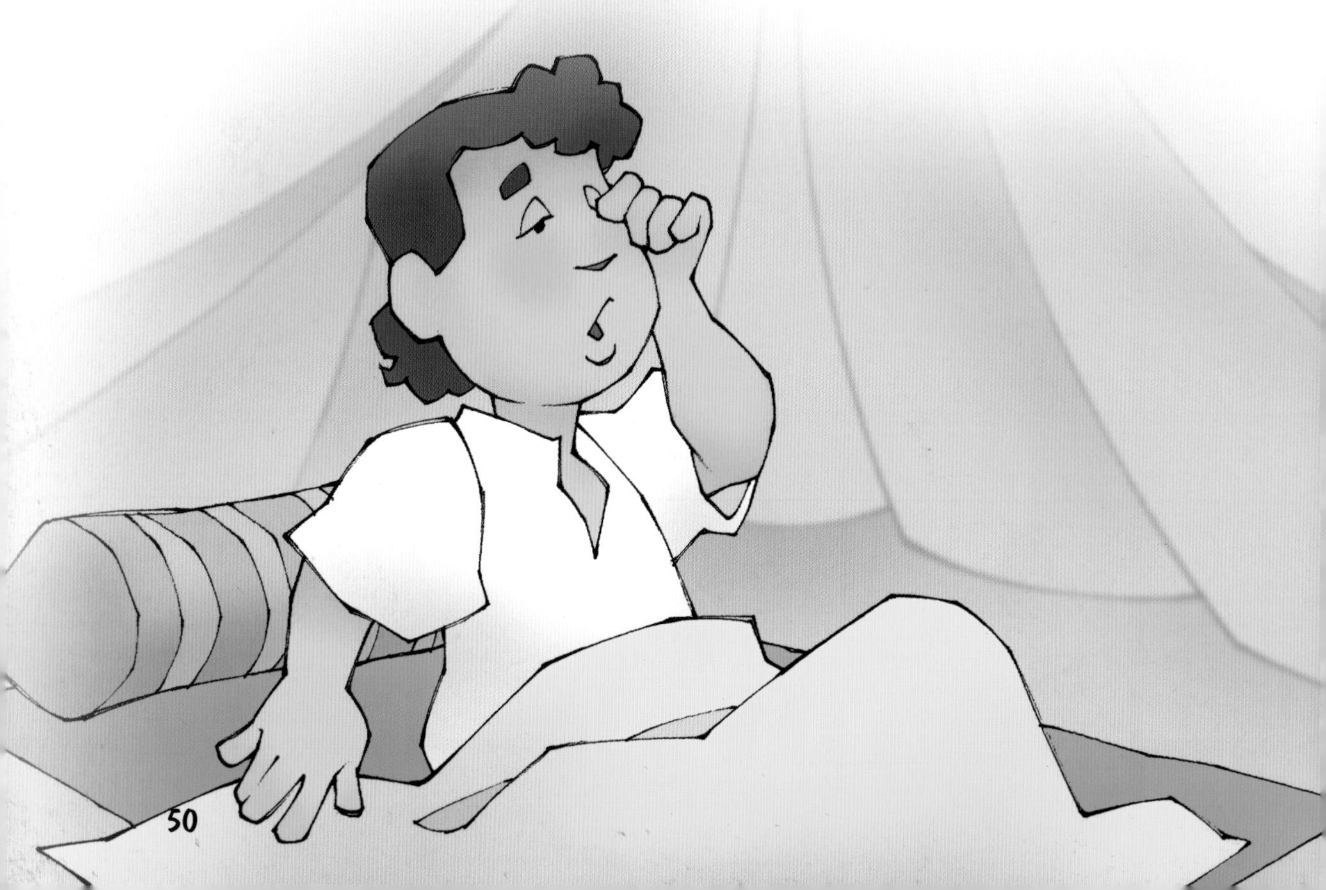

Eli had not called him. Samuel went back to bed.
Pretend to be sleeping.

Again the voice called, "Samuel!"

Samuel said, "Here I am."
Say, "Here I am."

It was not Eli calling. Samuel went back to bed.
Pretend to be sleeping.

51

A third time the voice called, "Samuel!"

Samuel said, "Here I am."

Say, "Here I am."

Eli knew it was God calling.

He told Samuel what to say.

God called again, "Samuel!"

Samuel said, "I'm listening, Lord."

Say, "I'm listening, Lord."

God gave Samuel a message for Eli.
Samuel listened to God and obeyed him.

Be quick to listen.
James 1:19, NLT

Samuel Chooses David as King

1 Samuel 16:1-13

God wanted to choose a new king for Israel.
So God told Samuel, "Go to Bethlehem and
find Jesse. One of his sons will be the new king.
I will show you the one."
Point to chest with thumb.

So Samuel went to Bethlehem.
He asked Jesse and his sons to come see him.
Jesse's son Eliab looked strong like a king.
Samuel nodded and said, "Surely he is the one."
Shake head yes.

But God said, "No! Don't judge by looks alone.
Samuel listened and said, "You're not the one."
Shake head no.

Then Jesse's son Abinadab walked before Samuel.
Samuel said, "You're not the one."
Shake head no.

Next, Jesse's son Shammah stepped forward.
Samuel shook his head and said,
"You're not the one."

Shake head no.

One by one, all seven of Jesse's sons came forward.
But each time Samuel said, "You're not the one."

Shake head no.

Samuel asked, "Are these all the sons you have?"
"There is still the youngest," Jesse said.
"He is out in the fields watching the sheep."
Samuel said, "He could be the one."

Hold hands out, palms up.

Jesse sent for David; he was handsome and
pleasant. The Lord knew David's heart. The
Lord said, "He is the one. Make him king."
This time Samuel said, "You are the one!"

Clap your hands.

God knows all hearts.
Proverbs 24:12, NLT

David and Goliath

1 Samuel 17:1-51

The people of Israel were at war.

March in place.

The enemies had a giant soldier named Goliath.

Stretch as tall as you can.

Goliath dared the soldiers, "Choose someone to come fight me."

Fold your arms across your chest.

But the soldiers of Israel were too scared.
Pretend to hide and look scared.

David was just a young shepherd boy. David told the king, "I will fight this giant." *Point to your chest.*

King Saul said, "But you are just a boy."
Shake your head and put hand out, palm down.

David said, "The Lord will take care of me."
Point upward.

David did not wear armor or carry a spear.
Shake head no.

He took his stick, a sling, and five stones.

Hold up five fingers.

Goliath laughed and then said,

"Am I a dog that you come with a stick?"

Put hands on your hips and pretend to laugh.

But David said, "Today the Lord will defeat you."

Point upward.

David hurled one stone from his sling.

Whirl your hand around your head.

The stone went flying through the air.
Trace the path with your hand.

It hit Goliath in the forehead.
Hit your forehead with your hand.

Goliath fell down to the ground.
Raise arms and then drop them.

Goliath was very dead!

God is our . . . protector.
Psalm 84:11, NLT

Jonathan Helps David

1 Samuel 18:1-4; 20:1-42

Jonathan was King Saul's son.

He and David promised to be best friends.

So Jonathan gave David a robe and many gifts.
  Pretend to give gifts.

The king didn't like David and wanted him dead.

"Why does he want me dead?" David asked.

"He does not want you killed," said Jonathan.
  Shake your head no.

David said, "Your father knows we are friends.

He would never tell you his plans."

But Jonathan agreed to help David.
  Nod head yes and pretend to shake hands.

Jonathan and David agreed on a secret signal.

David would hide in a field.

Jonathan would shoot three arrows.
Hold up three fingers.

"If I say, 'The arrows are right here,' you are OK.

But if I say, 'The arrows are over there,'

you are in danger and must leave," Jonathan said.
Point to a distant place.

Jonathan went to dinner with his father.

Saul was very angry that David was not there.

Saul even threw a spear at Jonathan.
Pretend to hide.

Jonathan went to the field where David
was hiding.

He shot three arrows far beyond David.

Jonathan shouted, "The arrows are over there!"
Pretend to shoot arrows.

David knew he had to run away from Saul.
The friends were very sad to say good-bye.
Jonathan said, "Go in peace.
We will be friends forever."

Pretend to wave good-bye.

A friend is always loyal.

Proverbs 17:17, NLT

King David and Mephibosheth

2 Samuel 9:1-13

 David had made a promise to his friend Jonathan. The king promised to care for Jonathan's family. David  for Jonathan's son. David wanted to show God's kindness to him. The son's name was

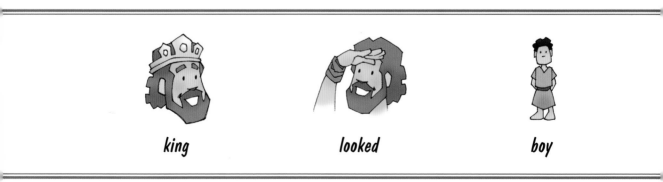

| king | looked | boy |

Mephibosheth. His 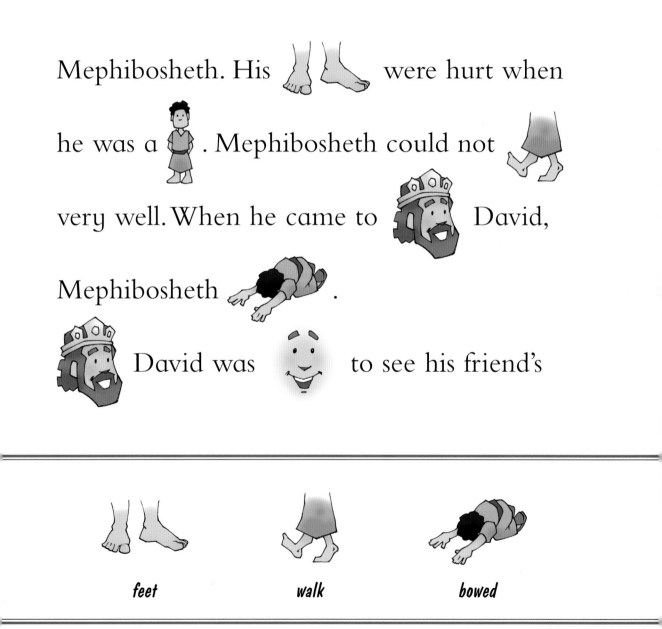 were hurt when he was a . Mephibosheth could not very well. When he came to David, Mephibosheth .

David was to see his friend's

feet   walk   bowed

son. "Don't be ," said David.

"I promised your father, Jonathan, that I would be kind to [you]." David gave Mephibosheth some [land] to farm.

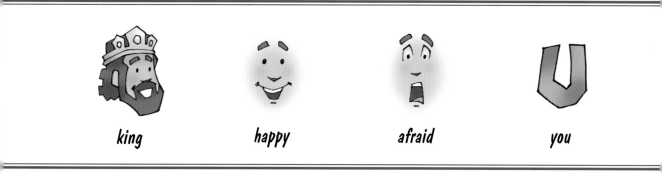

king   *happy*   *afraid*   *you*

 David told him, "live with me at the ." Mephibosheth ate at the king's .  David treated him like one of his own sons.

Show mercy and kindness to one another.
Zechariah 7:9, NLT

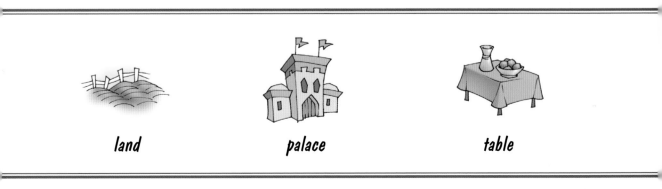

land palace table

Wise King Solomon

1 Kings 3:1-14

Solomon was the new king of Israel.
Put your hands on your head, fingers out, to make a crown.

Solomon loved God and prayed for help.
Fold fingers in prayer.

God talked to Solomon in a dream.
Put your fingers to your ear to listen.

God said, "Ask me for anything you want."
Open all your fingers, palms up.

Solomon said, "But I am like a child."
Point to yourself.

"Now I am to rule a nation with so many people."
Point your finger as if counting.

"Please give me wisdom so I can be a good king."
Point to your forehead.

God was happy with how Solomon answered.

Point your finger to your smiling face.

God said, "I will give you wisdom and riches and honor."

Cup your hands; pretend they are full of money.

Solomon praised God for his good gifts.

Lift hands up in praise.

72

Solomon became the wisest king ever.

Nod your head.

The people were happy with their new king.

Clap your hands.

Wisdom is better than silver.

Proverbs 3:14, NLT

73

God Cares for Elijah

1 Kings 16:29-33; 17:1-6

Bad king Ahab, bad king Ahab,
Didn't obey, didn't obey.
Ahab did not love God,
Ahab did not love God,
Not at all, not at all.

God sent Elijah, God sent Elijah,
Tell the king, tell the king.
Everything will dry up,
Everything will dry up,
No more rain, no more rain.

God told Elijah, God told Elijah,
Run and hide, run and hide.
By a brook with water,
By a brook with water,
You can drink, you can drink.

God fed Elijah, God fed Elijah,
Bread and meat, bread and meat.
Every day the food came,
Every day the food came,
From the birds, from the birds.

Your heavenly Father already knows all your needs.
Matthew 6:32, NLT

Elijah Goes to Heaven

2 Kings 2:1-15

Elisha went with Elijah and learned from him.

Elijah said, "Stay here, for I am going far away."
Point to the ground and then point far away.

But Elisha said, "I will never leave you."
Shake your head no.

Again Elijah said, "Stay here, for I am going far away."
Point to the ground and then point far away.

Again Elisha said, "I will never leave you."
Shake your head no.

Elijah and Elisha stopped by the Jordan River.
Pretend to walk and then stop.

Elijah hit the water with his folded cloak.
Pretend to hit the floor.

The river divided, and they crossed on dry ground.
Put your hands together, then move them apart.

Suddenly a chariot and horses of fire appeared!

Trot like a horse.

A strong wind took Elijah to heaven.

Make a wind sound and twirl your arm in circles.

Elisha watched Elijah go up to heaven.

Look upward.

Elisha picked up Elijah's cloak.

Pretend to pick up the cloak.

Then he hit the river with the cloak.

Pretend to hit the water.

The river divided and he walked on dry ground.

Put your hands together, then move them apart.

God's power was with Elisha.

Point upward.

With God's help we will do mighty things.

Psalm 60:12, NLT

Elisha and Namaan

2 Kings 5:1-15

Naaman was a soldier,

a strong and mighty soldier. **Use arms to make muscles.**

He won many battles, but Naaman was

very, very sick. **Lie down and look sick.**

No one could make him better.

Sad, sad Naaman. **Shake your head and look sad.**

His servant girl had an idea. A very good idea.
Point finger to head and nod.

The girl said, "God can heal you. Go see Elisha."
Pretend to be looking.

Naaman went to Elisha's house and
waited by the door. *Pretend to knock on door.*

Elisha's servant told Naaman, "Wash in the river."
Pretend to wash yourself.

Naaman was angry. "Why wash in that river?"
Pretend to stomp around.

But Naaman's officers said,

"You should obey Elisha." *Wag your finger back and forth.*

So Naaman went right into the Jordan River.
Pretend to be diving into water.

Naaman dipped himself seven times. Dip, dip, dip.
Dip up and down seven times.

Naaman was healed! His skin was smooth again!
Pretend to feel your skin.

Naaman said, "Now I know there is
one true God." *Point upward.*

The Lord will make them well.
James 5:15, NLT

85

SAY: *As I read the story, you do the motions.*

Daniel and His Friends

Daniel 1:1-21

Daniel was a young boy who lived in Jerusalem. One day some enemy soldiers came. They took Daniel and his friends to a faraway land.

Pretend to walk in place.

Daniel and his friends were taken to the king's palace. The young men were given the king's food and wine.

Pretend to set down food on a table.

Daniel and his friends did not want to eat the king's food. It was against God's rules.

Pretend to point to the food and shake head no.

Daniel said, "Give us only vegetables and water. See how we look after ten days. Then you can decide what we will eat."

Pretend to drink and eat.

So the king's official gave them vegetables and water. After ten days, Daniel and his friends looked the healthiest.

Pretend to look strong and healthy.

The king was pleased with Daniel and his friends. The four became the king's best helpers.

Make OK symbol with your fingers.

We must obey God.
Acts 5:29, NLT

Daniel and the Lions

Daniel 6:1-23

The king said, "Now pray to me,
Pray to me, pray to me."
The king said, "Now pray to me."
But Daniel prayed to God.

Daniel did not obey,
Not obey, not obey.
Daniel did not obey.
Throw him to the lions!

Daniel was not afraid,
Not afraid, not afraid.
Daniel was not afraid
Of the roaring lions!

An angel in the lions' den,
Lions' den, lions' den.
An angel in the lions' den,
Shut the lions' mouths.

Then the king was very pleased,
Very pleased, very pleased.
Then the king was very pleased
That God protected Daniel.

The LORD keeps watch over you.
Psalm 121:8, NLT

Jonah Learns to Obey

Jonah 1:1–3:3

God told Jonah to go to the

of Nineveh. He was to tell the about

God. Jonah did not want to go to the .

Jonah bought a to ride a .

city   people   ticket   boat

The  was sailing away from Nineveh.

There was a big ⛈ on the 🌊 .

The 👥 were afraid the ⛵ would

sink. Jonah knew that he had disobeyed God.

storm   **sea**   **sailors**

He said, "Throw me into the  ."

God sent a big 🐟 to save Jonah.

The 🐟 swallowed Jonah!

He was inside the fish for **3** days

and **3** nights.

Jonah 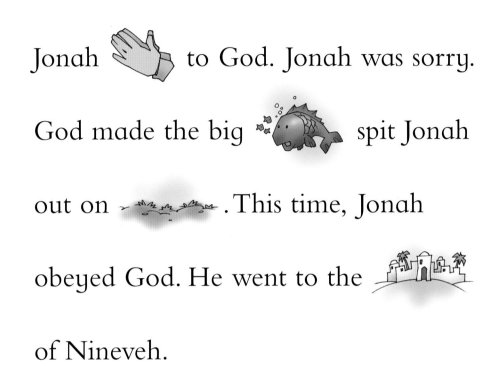 to God. Jonah was sorry.

God made the big spit Jonah

out on . This time, Jonah

obeyed God. He went to the

of Nineveh.

Obey his [God's] commands.

Ecclesiastes 12:13, NLT

prayed   **land**   **city**

An Angel Visits Zechariah

Luke 1:5-25, 57-64

and were very old.

They never had any children. One day

was serving in the Temple. Suddenly the angel

was standing there! "Don't be afraid!"

he said. "God heard your prayers.

Zechariah　　　　　　*Elizabeth*

"You and your wife Elizabeth will have a son.

You are to name him . You will have

great joy!" did not believe .

"How can I know this will happen?"

asked. "I am an old man now, and my

Gabriel   **John**

"wife is old, too."  said, "You do not believe me! Now you won't talk until is born." tried to talk. But he could not say one word. Later  had a baby boy. People wanted to call him .

Zechariah

Elizabeth

said, "No! His name is . They

asked what name he wanted.

wrote, "His name is ." Just then

 could talk again! "Praise the Lord,

the God of Israel," exclaimed  .

With God everything is possible.
Matthew 19:26, NLT

Gabriel

John

SING this story to the tune of "Jingle Bells."

Jesus Is Born

Luke 2:1-20

Baby boy, baby boy,
Sleeping in the hay.
Oh, the baby Jesus,
Born on Christmas day.

Happy song, happy song,
Angels sang out loud.
Oh, the shepherds were amazed
At the heavenly throng!

Shepherds ran, shepherds ran,
Running all the way.
Coming to see Jesus,
To worship him and pray.

Shepherds told, shepherds told,
Everyone their joy,
That a Savior had been born,
A little baby boy!

The Savior . . . has been born tonight in Bethlehem.
Luke 2:11, NLT

The Wise Men Visit Jesus

Matthew 2:1-12

Some wise men saw a special star.

Point upward.

So they jumped on their camels.

Jump, landing with legs apart.

They followed the star. Bump, bump, bump.

Bounce up and down at your knees.

They rode night and day.

Pretend to be riding a donkey.

God's star showed the way to go.
Point upward.

The wise men stopped in Jerusalem
to see the king. *Make a crown with your hands.*

"We are looking for the new king," they said.
Shade eyes with hand and look around.

The king did not like what he heard.
Stomp around.

His teachers looked in their books.
Put your hands together to make an open book.

The teachers told the wise men to go to
Bethlehem. *Point forward.*

So they followed the star again.
Bump, bump, bump.
Bounce up and down on your knees.

The star stopped over the place where Jesus was.
Touch fingertips of hands to form a roof.

The wise men jumped from their camels.
Jump, landing with legs together.

They were so happy to see Jesus!
Clap your hands.

The wise men worshiped Jesus.
Kneel and fold your hands.

And they gave beautiful gifts to the baby.
Lay gifts on the floor.

We have come to worship him [Jesus].
Matthew 2:2, NLT

109

Jesus Is Baptized

Mark 1:1-11

John was a special messenger from God.
> *Point upward and then point to mouth.*

John lived in the wilderness.
> *Point to a distant spot.*

And he wore camel hair clothes.
> *Touch your clothes.*

John ate locusts and wild honey.
> *Pretend to eat.*

He told people to ask God for forgiveness.
> *Fold your hands as if praying.*

Then he baptized them in the river.
> *Cup one hand and pretend to pour water.*

John said, "Someone greater is coming."
> *Reach both arms up high.*

One day Jesus came to the river.

Make your fingers walk.

John baptized Jesus in the river.

Cup one hand and pretend to pour water.

The heavens split open.

Put your hands together, then move them apart.

Like a dove, the Holy Spirit came down.

Move your fingers like a bird flying.

A voice called from heaven.

Put your hands around your mouth.

God said, "This is my Son, whom I love."

This [Jesus] is my beloved Son.
Matthew 17:5, NLT

Jesus Calls His Followers

Luke 5:1-11

One day Jesus was preaching by the  .

He stepped into Simon's 🛶 by the shore.

Jesus talked to the 👥 from the 🛶 .

Then Jesus said, "Sail out into the ☁️ .

Let down your 🪢 in the deep water.

---

sea   boat   people

"You will catch lots and lots of  ."

Simon said, "Master, we worked all night.

And we didn't catch even one  .

But if you say so, we will try again."

This time their  were filled with  !

water   nets   fish

So many  they had to shout for help!

And another came to help them.

2 boats were filled with  !

Simon was so amazed he fell to his knees.

He knew Jesus was the Son of God.

fish   boat

His friends, James and John, were also amazed.

But Jesus said, "Don't be ! Follow me

and be my helpers. From now on you will

for people." Simon and his friends

quickly followed Jesus.

[Jesus said] . . . "Follow me."
John 21:19, NLT

two   afraid

Jesus Heals a Paralyzed Man

Mark 2:1-12

Jesus was teaching in a house.

Many people came to see Jesus. Full, full house.
Pretend you are in a crowd trying to see.

Four men came carrying a man on a mat.

The man on the mat could not walk at all.
Shake your head no.

They knew Jesus could heal their friend.

So they went to the house, but they couldn't get in.
Pretend to knock on the door.

The four men climbed up to the roof.

Then they dug a hole in the roof. Dig, men, dig!
Pretend to dig with your hands.

Slowly, they lowered their friend down.

Down, down he went. Right in front of Jesus.
Pretend to lower the mat.

Jesus said, "Your sins are forgiven."
Some people got angry.
"Only God can forgive sins!"
Stomp your feet and shake your fist.
Jesus said, "I will prove that I have power to forgive."
He told the man, "You are healed! Get up and walk!" *Pretend to jump up and walk.*

The man jumped up! He took his mat and left. The people said,

"We've never seen anything like this."

Shout "Thank you, Jesus!"

He [God] forgives all my sins.
Psalm 103:3, NLT

Jesus Calms a Storm

Mark 4:35-41

It was night, and Jesus said to his helpers,

"Let's take the boat across the lake."

The lake was dark, deep, and quiet.
   Make a ssshhh! sound.

The helpers started to row.

Soon a fierce storm broke out.
   Make noise like wind and thunder.

Big waves splashed into their boat,

nearly filling the boat with water!
   Make noise like crashing waves.

Jesus was in the back of the boat.

But he was sound asleep.
   Pretend to snore.

Jesus' helpers woke him up with a shout.

"Don't you even care if we drown?"
   Shout "Wake up! Wake up!"

Jesus stood up and looked about.

Then he told the storm, "Quiet down!"
Make a ssshh! noise.

The wind stopped. The waves stopped.

And the lake was as calm as it could be.
Make a sound like the wind, then get quiet.

"Why are you so afraid?" Jesus asked.

"Do you still not have faith in me?"
Say, "Why are you so afraid?"

Jesus' helpers said, "Who is this man?

Even the wind and the waves obey him."
Make a sound like the wind.

Don't be troubled or afraid.
John 14:27, NLT

Jesus Feeds the People

John 6:1-14

Rowing across the sea. Row, men, row.
Pretend to row the boat.

Climbing a big hill. Climb, Jesus, climb.
Pretend to climb a big hill.

Seeing a crowd of people. A big, big crowd.
Move both arms in wide, sweeping motions.

Sitting on the grass. The cool, cool grass.
Sit on the floor. Pat the floor.

Asking his friends, "Where can we buy food?"
Throw hands up as if asking a question.

Sharing a boy's lunch. Five loaves, two fish.
Hold up five fingers and two fingers.

Jesus prays for the food. Thanks, God, thanks!
Fold hands and bow head.

Passing out the food. Everyone eats!
Pretend to eat.

Picking up the leftovers. Lots and lots of food.
Pretend to pick up pieces and put in baskets.

Jesus is God's Son. Great, great news.
Raise both arms upward.

God will . . . provide all you need.
2 Corinthians 9:8, NLT

Jesus Walks on Water

Mark 6:45-51

Jesus sent his helpers across the lake in the boat.
Make your hand go back and forth gently like a wave.

Then he went up into the hills near the lake.
Make a hill with your fingertips.

He wanted to be by himself to pray.
Fold your hands.

During the night, the wind became very strong.
Cup your hands by your mouth and blow.

The boat was rocked up and down by the waves.

Cup your hands and rock them back and forth.

Jesus' helpers were in trouble.

Pretend to be scared.

They rowed and rowed!

Paddle with your hands.

Jesus walked to them on top of the water.
Walk with your fingers.

When his helpers saw Jesus, they screamed!
Cover mouth as if to scream.

They thought he was a ghost.
Cover your eyes with your hands.

Jesus said, "I am here. Don't be afraid."
Pat yourself on the back.

Then Jesus climbed into the boat.
Cup one hand, climb into it with your fingers.

The wind and the waves stopped.
Hold your hand up; palm facing out.

Jesus has power over everything!
Give a thumbs-up.

The earth is the LORD's, and everything in it.
Psalm 24:1, NLT

133

The Good Samaritan

Luke 10:30-37

One day Jesus told this story: A Jewish man was walking along a dusty road. *Walk in place.*

Suddenly, some robbers jumped out from behind the rocks. *Jump and pretend to scare someone.*

They hit the man until he was almost dead. *Punch the air with both fists.*

Then they took his money and clothes. *Pretend to grab things and run off.*

And the man was left lying by the road.

Curl up in a ball like you're hurt.

Soon a Jewish priest came walking by.

Walk in place.

But the priest did not stop to help.

Extend arm, hand out, palm out, and shake your head no.

A Temple helper walked over to the man.

Walk in place, look at the floor.

But the Temple worker did not stop to help.

Extend arm, hand out, palm out, and shake your head no.

Then a Samaritan man came along.
Walk in place.

He felt sad and stopped to help the man.
Kneel down on the floor.

The Samaritan put medicine and bandages
on his sores. *Pretend to put bandages on your arm.*

Then the Samaritan put the hurt man
on his donkey. *Pretend to lead a donkey.*

He took the hurt man to an inn
and cared for him. *Pretend to knock on a door.*

The Samaritan paid the innkeeper for a room.
Pretend to put money in your hand.

Jesus asked, "Who was a good neighbor?"
Hold your hand up as if asking a question.

Someone answered, "The man who helped."

"Yes," Jesus said. "Now go and do the same."

Love your neighbor as yourself.
Matthew 19:19, NLT

Mary and Martha

Luke 10:38-42

Jesus went to visit Mary and Martha.

Martha welcomed him into the house.
Pretend to open the door and wave hello.

Mary and Martha were very happy to
see Jesus. There was so much to do!
Clap your hands.

Martha was busy sweeping the floor.
Pretend to be sweeping the floor.

Her sister Mary sat at Jesus' feet.
Pretend to look at Mary, hands on hip, shaking head.

Martha was busy fixing dinner.
Pretend to be cooking dinner.

Her sister Mary sat at Jesus' feet.
Pretend to look at Mary, hands on hip, shaking head.

Martha was busy setting the table.
Pretend to be setting the table.

Her sister Mary sat at Jesus' feet.
Pretend to look at Mary, hands on hip, shaking head.

139

Finally, Martha said, "It's not fair, Jesus!"
Stand with hands on hip, shaking head.

"I am busy doing all the work and Mary just sits.
Tell her to come help me."
Pretend to point at Mary.

Jesus said, "My dear Martha. You are so worried."
Pretend to look away.

"There is really only one thing that's important. Mary already knows what it is. She is taking time to be with me," Jesus said.

Sit down and pretend to listen to Jesus.

Take delight in the LORD.
Psalm 37:4, NLT

141

Ten Sick Men

Luke 17:11-19

Ten men sat by a road near town.
They were very sick with leprosy.
Jesus can help us.

142

Leprosy was a terrible disease.

No one could make the men well.

Jesus can help us.

The sick men saw Jesus walking by.

The men cried, "Have mercy on us!"

They believed Jesus could make them well.

Jesus can help us.

Jesus said, "Go see the priests now."

And as they went, their leprosy disappeared!

Jesus can help us.

One man came back to Jesus.

He fell on his knees and thanked Jesus.

"Praise God, I am healed!" he said.

Jesus can help us.

"Didn't I heal ten men?" Jesus asked.

"Where are the other nine?

Does only one return to say thank you?"

Jesus can help us.

Jesus said to the man, "Stand up and go.

Your faith has made you well."

Give thanks for everything to God.
Ephesians 5:20, NLT

Jesus and the Children

Mark 10:13-16

Little, little girls and boys,

Wanting to see Jesus.

Coming with their moms and dads.

Coming with their hearts so glad.

Little, little girls and boys,

Wanting to see Jesus.

Little, little girls and boys,

Wanting to see Jesus.

But his friends said, "Go away.

Do not bother him today."

Little, little girls and boys,

Wanting to see Jesus.

Little, little girls and boys,
Wanting to see Jesus.
Jesus said, "Oh, let them be.
Let them come and sit with me."
Little, little girls and boys,
Wanting to see Jesus.

Little, little girls and boys,
Wanting to see Jesus.
Jesus touched them on their heads.
Blessed each one, and then he said,
"Little, little girls and boys,
Always come; you bring me joy."

[Jesus said] . . . "Let the children come to me."
Mark 10:14, NLT

149

Jesus and Bartimaeus

Mark 10:46-52

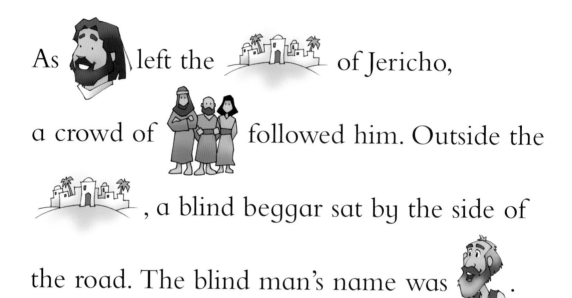

As left the of Jericho, a crowd of followed him. Outside the , a blind beggar sat by the side of the road. The blind man's name was .

Bartimaeus

city

When  heard that was nearby,

he shouted, " , have mercy on me!"

"Be quiet!" the yelled at him.

But just shouted louder. stopped

Jesus   people

when he heard  shouting. "Tell him to come here," said. "Come on," the said. "He's calling you!" Then jumped up and came to . "What do you want?"

Jesus

people

asked. said, "I want to see!"

"Your faith has healed you," said.

Right away could see! was so

excited! He followed down the road.

The LORD hears his people.
Psalm 34:17, NLT

Bartimaeus

Jesus and Zacchaeus

Luke 19:1-10

Zacchaeus was a tax collector.

Pretend to count money.

Zacchaeus did not have many friends.

Shake your head no.

He heard Jesus was coming to his town.

Put your hand behind your ear to listen.

Zacchaeus wanted to see Jesus.

Shade your eyes with your hand.

But Zacchaeus was a very short man.
Stoop down low.

He couldn't see Jesus over the crowd.
Stand on tiptoe and stretch to see.

So Zacchaeus climbed a tree by the side
of the road. *Pretend to climb a tree.*

From way up high he could see everything.
Lean over and look down.

Jesus walked by and looked up at Zacchaeus.
Look up.

"Zacchaeus," he said. "Quick, come down."
Reach hand up and motion to come.

"I want to go to your house."
Clap your hands.

Zacchaeus was so excited he quickly
climbed down! *Pretend to climb down the tree.*

"I'm sorry for cheating people," Zacchaeus said.
Hang your head down.

"I will give all the money back to them."
Pretend to hand out money.

Jesus knew that Zacchaeus had changed and
forgave him. *Shake your head yes.*

There is forgiveness for your sins.
Acts 13:38, NLT

Jesus Enters Jerusalem

Matthew 21:1-11

Jesus and his helpers were near Jerusalem.
Jesus sent two helpers into a town nearby.
"You will find a donkey there," Jesus said.
"Untie it and bring it to me."
The helpers took the donkey to Jesus.
They put their coats on the donkey's back.
Then Jesus got on the donkey and rode.

158

A crowd quickly surrounded him.

Hosanna to the King! *Pretend to look for Jesus.*

People spread their coats on the road.

Hosanna to the King! *Pretend to put your coat on the road.*

Others put palm branches on the road.

Hosanna to the King! *Pretend to put a palm branch on the road.*

Some waved branches in the air.

Hosanna to the King! *Pretend to wave a palm branch in the air.*

Jesus rode the donkey into the city.

Hosanna to the King! *Pretend to wave and watch Jesus go by.*

The people shouted and praised God.

Hosanna to the King! *Pump your fist into the air.*

The people were happy to see Jesus.
Hosanna to the King! *Jump and clap.*
They welcomed him like a king.
Hosanna to the King! *Pretend to bow down before a king.*

Bless the King!
Luke 19:38, NLT

161

A Special Dinner

John 13:1-17

Jesus knew that he would die soon.
It was time for him to return to his Father.
He ate one last dinner with his helpers.
Pretend to eat.

162

After dinner, Jesus got up from the table.

He took off his robe.

Pretend to take off a robe.

He tied a towel around his waist.

Pretend to tie a towel around your waist.

Then Jesus poured water into a bowl.

Pretend to pour water into a bowl.

Jesus began to wash his helpers' feet.
Kneel down and pretend to wash feet.

He wiped them with the towel.
Pretend to wipe the feet dry.

Jesus washed all his helpers' feet.

Then he put his robe back on.
Pretend to put a robe on.

"Do you understand what I was doing?"
Jesus asked.
Hold your hands out as if asking a question.

"You must wash each other's feet.

Follow my example and show your love by

serving each other."
Pretend to serve someone.

Follow God's example in everything you do.
Ephesians 5:1, NLT

Jesus' Trial and Death

Luke 23:1-46

The leaders took Jesus to the governor.
Make your fingers walk.

The leaders said, "This man claims to be a king."
With your fingers, make a crown on your head.

The governor asked, "Are you a king?"

Jesus said, "Yes, it is as you say."
Hold hands together and nod yes.

The governor said Jesus had done nothing wrong.
Hold both hands out, palms out.

So the soldiers took Jesus to King Herod.
Make your fingers walk.

King Herod asked Jesus many questions.

But Jesus refused to answer and said nothing.
Put your hand over your mouth.

The soldiers made fun of Jesus and mocked him.
Wag your finger.

Then the soldiers took Jesus back to the governor.
Make your fingers walk.

Again, the governor said Jesus had done nothing wrong. *Shake head, hold both hands out, palms out.*

But the people shouted, "Kill him! Kill him!"
Shake fists.

Finally, the governor said, "Take Jesus away."
Make shooing motions with hands.

The soldiers led Jesus to the cross.
Make your fingers walk.

Jesus was nailed to the cross and died.
Point a finger into each palm.

Jesus died for the sins of all people.
Fold hands and say, "Thank you, Jesus."

He [Jesus] died for our sins.
Galatians 1:4, NLT

Jesus Is Alive

John 20:1-18

It was early Sunday morning. Very, very early.
Stretch and yawn.

Mary came to the tomb. The tomb of Jesus.
Walk in place.

The stone was rolled away! Who moved it?
Pretend to look around.

Mary hurried away. Run, Mary, run.
Pretend to run in place.

She found Peter and John. Told them the news.

Pretend to talk excitedly.

"Jesus' body is gone!" Where can it be?

Pretend to be looking for something.

Peter and John ran to the tomb. Run, run, run.

Pretend to run in place.

They looked in the tomb. Where was Jesus?

Pretend to look inside.

Mary stayed at the tomb. Crying big tears.
Pretend to be crying.

Then Mary saw a man. Was he the gardener?
Pretend to look up.

The man asked Mary, "Why are you crying?"

Mary said, "I'm looking for Jesus. Where is he?"
Hold hands out and shake head as if asking a question.

172

The man said, "Mary!" He was Jesus!

Mary shouted, "Teacher!" Happy, happy Mary.
Clap your hands.

Mary ran to tell everyone. Run, Mary, run.
Pretend to run in place.

"I have seen the Lord!" Mary said. Jesus is alive!

Christ died and rose again.
Romans 14:9, NLT

The Road to Emmaus

Luke 24:13-31

2 of Jesus' helpers were walking.

came up and walked with them.

The did not know .

asked, "What are you talking about?"

They said, "We are talking about .

---

two

Jesus

helpers

"He did many wonderful things. But  was put to death on a ✝. Today some women went to the tomb. They saw some angels at the tomb." The angels told them that Jesus is alive!

cross   women   angels

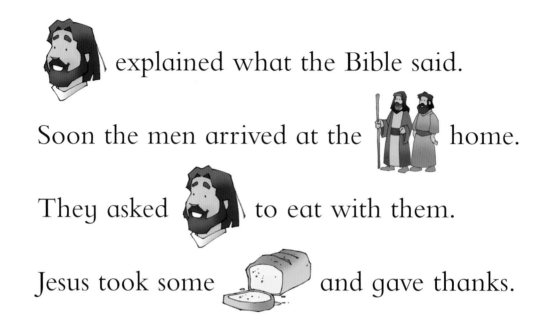

explained what the Bible said.

Soon the men arrived at the home.

They asked to eat with them.

Jesus took some and gave thanks.

Jesus

helpers

He broke the  and gave it to them.

Then the helpers knew he was .

At that moment,  disappeared!

[Jesus said] . . . "Look, I am alive forever and ever!"
Revelation 1:18, NLT

bread

Breakfast by the Sea

John 21:1-14

Fish, fish, fish all night,
Catching not a one.
The men were ready to give up
Until they saw someone.

"Fish, fish, fish again,
Throw your nets once more.
You'll be glad if you obey.
Your nets will hold no more."

Swim, swim, swim ashore.
Peter understood.
It was Jesus standing there.
Life was now so good.

Cook, cook, cook the fish;
Such a breakfast treat.
Jesus with his friends again,
Serving fish to eat.

[Jesus said] . . ."I will see you again; then you will rejoice."
John 16:22, NLT

Jesus Returns to Heaven

Acts 1:3-12

Many people saw Jesus after he rose from the dead.
Shade eyes with hand; look all around.

One day Jesus walked up onto a hill.
Pretend to climb up a hill.

He took his helpers with him.
Make a motion to come.

"Wait for the Holy Spirit," Jesus said.
Link thumbs, move hands in a bird motion.

"Then you will tell other people about me."
Cup your hands around your mouth.

"You will tell about me all over the world."
Move your hands in wide sweeping motions.

His helpers were listening and watching Jesus.
Shade eyes with hand.

Then Jesus began to rise up into the sky!
Spread arms out at sides, stand on tiptoe.

He disappeared into a cloud.
Arch your arms over your head.

The helpers kept looking up into the sky.
Shade eyes with hands and look up.

Suddenly two angels were beside them.
Look surprised.

"Why are you staring at the sky?" they asked.

Point toward the sky.

"Jesus will come back some day."

Point upward, slowly bring hand down.

Then Jesus' helpers went back to the city.

Walk in place.

[Jesus said] . . . "I am with you always."

Matthew 28:20, NLT

Saul Sees Jesus

Acts 9:1-20

 did not believe in .

He wanted to put Jesus' followers in  .

One day was going to Damascus.

Suddenly he saw a bright . fell

down on the .

Saul   Jesus   jail

186

A voice said, "  , why are you hurting me?"

asked, "Who are you?" answered,

"I am the one you are hurting. Now go into

the city and do what you are told." When

got up, he could not see.

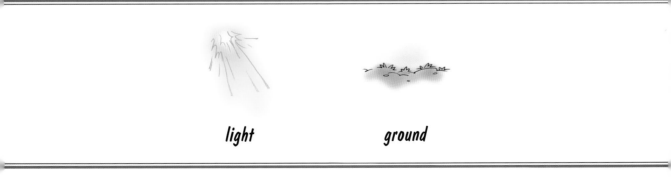

light *ground*

He could not see for  3 days. wanted Ananias to help Saul. But Ananias had heard bad things about Saul. Jesus said, "I chose Saul to be my helper." So Ananias put his hands on Saul's eyes.

Saul

three

"  sent me to help you," he said.

Right away could see again!

Then he was baptized by Ananias.

 became a follower of .

[Jesus said] . . . "Tell people about me everywhere."
Acts 1:8, NLT

Jesus   **hands**

Paul and Silas in Prison

Acts 16:16-34

Paul and Silas were telling others about Jesus.

But some people became angry at what they said.

Pretend to be talking.

The angry men had Paul and Silas arrested.

Paul and Silas were put in jail.

Pretend to walk as if in chains.

190

In jail, Paul and Silas still trusted Jesus.

They prayed and sang songs to God.
Pretend to sing and pray.

At midnight God sent a big earthquake.

It shook the jail, and the doors flew open!
Pretend to shake and act frightened.

The chains fell off all the prisoners.

Pretend to be free from chains.

The jailer was afraid that everyone escaped.

He was going to kill himself.

Paul said, "Don't do it! We are all here."

Pretend to point as if others are in the room.

The jailer asked, "How can I be saved?"

Paul and Silas said, "Believe in Jesus."

Point upward.

The jailer took them to his home.

His whole family believed in Jesus.

Paul and Silas baptized them all.

Pretend to baptize.

The joy of the LORD is your strength.
Nehemiah 8:10, NLT

Paul and His Nephew

Acts 23:12-31

Paul was a prisoner in an army jail.

Some angry men wanted to kill Paul.

They made plans to capture Paul.

But Paul's nephew heard of their plan.

And he went to the jail and told Paul.

Paul   jail   nephew

 called one of the to come to him.

He said, "Take my to the .

He has something important to tell him."

So the took Paul's nephew to the .

The took Paul's aside.

officers   commander

The  told him of the men's plan.

He said, "Some  want to kill  .

They are going to ask you to move .

The are going to hide along the road.

nephew   angry men

"Then they are going to jump on  and kill him." The believed

Paul's . was moved to a

safer place.

Let your good deeds shine.
Matthew 5:16, NLT

Paul

commander

Paul Is Shipwrecked

Acts 27:1-44

Roman soldiers had arrested Paul.

Stand straight, pretend to hold a spear.

Paul was on a prison ship going to Rome.

Rock back and forth like a ship on the sea.

The sea was rough, and the wind was cold.

Pretend you are cold.

Paul said, "We should not keep on sailing."

Shake your head.

"The ship might sink and everyone will be hurt."

Smash one fist into your other hand.

No one listened to Paul. They kept sailing.

Put your hands over your ears.

Soon a terrible storm began to blow.

Pretend to be blown around by the wind.

It rained and rained for many, many days.

Use your fingers to make raindrops fall.

The people on the ship were very afraid.
Look scared, hold your head.

They threw everything over the side of the ship.
Pretend to throw things overboard.

Paul said, "Be brave. An angel visited me."
Point upward.

"God said we will all be safe."
Look upward and hug yourself.

"But the ship will be wrecked."
Smash one fist into your other hand.

Soon the ship was close to land and crashed.
Hand above eyes, look toward land.

Some people swam to the land.
Make swimming motions.

Others held onto boards and floated to the land.
Stretch arms outward as if floating.

God kept everyone safe, just as Paul had said!
Point upward.

The LORD protects me from danger.
Psalm 27: 1, NLT

SAY: Help me tell this story by repeating, "Heaven is a wonderful place."

A Wonderful Place

Revelation 21:1-27

John was a prisoner on an island. He was put on the island for talking about Jesus. One day he had a vision about heaven.

Heaven is a wonderful place.

He saw a beautiful holy city—God's home.
Heaven is a wonderful place.

The city shone and sparkled like gold.
Heaven is a wonderful place.

The walls were filled with jewels.
Heaven is a wonderful place.

The twelve gates were made of pearls.
Heaven is a wonderful place.

Heaven is where people live with God.
Heaven is a wonderful place.

In heaven, we will be happy and never sad.
Heaven is a wonderful place.

There will be no crying or pain in heaven.
Heaven is a wonderful place.

The sun and moon are not needed in heaven.
Heaven is a wonderful place.

The glory of God lights up heaven.
Heaven is a wonderful place.

Heaven is where we will live forever with Jesus.
Heaven is a wonderful place.

[Jesus said] . . . "I am going to prepare a place for you."
John 14:2, NLT

Memory Verse Index

Here is a list of memory verses printed with each Bible story
from the New Living Translation.

THE NLT™ STORY BIBLE SERIES

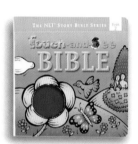

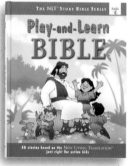

Seven Books, Seven Reasons.

The NLT™ Story Bible Series is the easy choice. Here's why:

 Reason 1
It covers every age and stage of your child's development.

It grows with your child from birth to twelve. **Reason 2**

 Reason 3
The NLT™ is today's most popular new Bible version.

It's easy for your child to understand because the NLT™ is user-friendly. **Reason 4**

 Reason 5
It's easy for you to choose just the right book for your child.

It was developed with input from best-selling author and child development expert Dr. Mary Manz Simon. **Reason 6**

 Reason 7
It's published by Standard Publishing, the leader in children's Bible storybooks.

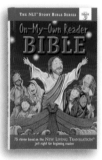

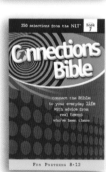

Word-and-Picture Bible
Item no: 04141
ISBN: 0-7847-1594-7

Touch-and-See Bible
Item no: 04142
ISBN: 0-7847-1595-5

Flap-and-Tab Bible
Item no: 04143
ISBN: 0-7847-1596-3

Play-and-Learn Bible
Item no: 04144
ISBN: 0-7847-1597-1

On-My-Own Reader Bible
Item no: 04145
ISBN: 0-7847-1598-X

One Way Bible
Item no: 04146
ISBN: 0-7847-1599-8

Connections Bible
Item no: 04147
ISBN: 0-7847-1500-9

S
Standard PUBLISHING

www.standardpub.com